What people are saying about ...

TOUCHING WONDER

"In this collection of short readings for advent, John Blase helps us encounter the Christmas story ... with dirt beneath its fingernails. This is the incarnation as real as it gets, God-with-us in all our fleshly despair and hope. Smell the hay in the Bethlehem stable, soaked with birthing blood. Hear Mary's pants and cries as she pushes the living God from her womb. Look over Joseph's shoulder as he watches his beloved bear the child of Another, the Son he will raise who will raise all humankind. Hear the duet of adoration from Anna and Simeon as they witness the fulfillment of the promise of the ages. Read *Touching Wonder*, and remind yourself once again of the absurd, unexpected, unfathomable glory of God's arrival in our world."

Thom Lemmons, author of *Blameless*

"John Blase writes evocatively, passionately, and beautifully. This creative series of sketches and letters makes the familiar fresh and brings us to the inside of the Christmas event. A delight."

Andrew Wilson, author of
GodStories and *Incomparable*

"With a poet's gift for seeing into and depicting the heart of a scene, John Blase leads us through the birth of Christ. With Blase, we hear the voices of the story in fresh, authentic, and powerful new ways so that we're startled, amazed, and grateful all over again."

Joy Jordan-Lake, author of
Blue Hole Back Home and *Why Jesus Makes Me Nervous*

"Recovering wonder is never easy. But John Blase provides a doorway through his graceful book, *Touching Wonder.* The anticipation meant for advent is often lost in the very season when steady pacing, taking time, and breathing deeply ought to be its hallmarks. John Blase gives us that unhurried time back by expanding on the human side of the Christ child's heritage, the men and women who were there before and after His birth giving us living examples of how the Scripture speaks to us in contemporary ways. Eugene Peterson's *The Message* coupled with John's tender stories and singular prayers makes this a book I will read again and again."

Jane Kirkpatrick, award-winning author of *A Sweetness to the Soul* and *A Flickering Light*

"We need to be surprised again. We need to gasp, to be amazed, to hear as if for the first time. We need to be curious, to imagine, to cry and dance. All that is to say: We need true storytellers. Thank God, in John Blase, we have one."

Winn Collier, author of *Restless Faith* and *Holy Curiosity*, www.winncollier.com

"This powerfully realized, intimate report of the happenings of the incarnation shows how human imagination (John Blase's) can illuminate what, without faith, has always seemed impossible, incredible. The whole Christ-event is a demonstration of how the transcendent and the immanent meet in human bodies and souls that are wide open to God-work—ordinary people willing to undergo the unthinkable. Blase's vivid telling of the story, based on Eugene Peterson's rendering of Luke, thrusts us into the heart of the action in memorable ways. Tradition may have dulled the images we remember during advent. This retelling imbues them with startling life."

Luci Shaw, poet and author
of *Accompanied by Angels* and
Breath for the Bones, and Writer
in Residence, Regent College

"John Blase has smoothly moved back through the razor-wire of secular noels and arrived at the great simplicity of things as they were before Rudolph and Frosty and the Grinch. Mind you I'm not opposed to the trio, it's just that Luke so often can't get the incarnation of our Lord through the tangle of mistletoe and sleigh bells to the bare barn floor of the greater truths fanned by angels wings on that wonderful night when God learned the art of whimpering for His next meal. I say God bless you,

John Blase, for rigging advent in the direction of reality and hope. Your venture is most welcome!"

Calvin Miller, Distinguished Writer
in Residence, Beeson Divinity School

"John Blase positions himself at the epicenter of the Bethlehem Bomb and lets the shock waves shake, rattle, and roll us through art, poetry, prayers, reflections, and Scripture. The magic of a musical 'Winter Wonderland' is nothing compared to the wonder of this so-beautiful 'Four Seasons Wonderland.'"

Leonard Sweet, Drew University,
George Fox Evangelical
Seminary, www.sermons.com

"Our wrapping paper and lawn balloon-snowmen literally fade when reading John's rich and penetrating description of the absurd, fierce, quiet, comical, and loving rescue of humanity. Thank you, John. You made me love Christmas."

Jan Meyers, author of *The Allure
of Hope* and *Listening to Love*

"Blase writes with an honest confessional earthiness seldom found among Christian authors. He writes from the genre of his soul bared out on ink and paper, and brings the reader into the drama of the advent / Christmas story. *Touching Wonder* brings new breath to a story we thought we knew so well. This engaging work of both the divine heart of God and the earthly heart of Blase will be sure to bring you to the manger with a new understanding of Christmas."

Reverend Tyg Taylor, pastor of Trinity
Lutheran Church, Monument, CO

"I've always loved the way some writers can rescue biblical narrative from all the thees and thous and make it real for us. John Blase has certainly done that with *Touching Wonder*. This is one of the few Christmas-themed books (out of millions this time of year) that I would actually recommend."

Pierce Pettis, recording
artist and songwriter

TOUCHING
WONDER

TOUCHING
WONDER

Recapturing the Awe
of Christmas

JOHN BLASE

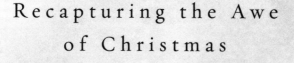

transforming lives together

TOUCHING WONDER
Published by David C. Cook
4050 Lee Vance View
Colorado Springs, CO 80918 U.S.A.

David C. Cook Distribution Canada
55 Woodslee Avenue, Paris, Ontario, Canada N3L 3E5

David C. Cook U.K., Kingsway Communications
Eastbourne, East Sussex BN23 6NT, England

David C. Cook and the graphic circle C logo
are registered trademarks of Cook Communications Ministries.

Scripture quotations are from *THE MESSAGE*. Copyright ©
by Eugene H. Peterson 1993, 1994, 1995, 1996, 2000, 2001,
2002. Used by permission of NavPress Publishing Group.
"Recognition" © Luci Shaw. Used by permission.

LCCN 2009928003
ISBN 978-1-4347-6465-2

© 2009 John Blase

Published in association with the literary agency
of Alive Communications, Inc, 7680 Goddard St.,
Suite 200, Colorado Springs, CO 80920

The Team: Brian Thomasson, Karen Lee-
Thorp, Caitlyn York, Karen Athen

Cover Design: Amy Kiechlin
Cover Images: iStockphoto
Interior Illustrations: Amanda Jolman

Printed in Canada
First Edition 2009

2 3 4 5 6 7 8 9 10 11

092509

FOR DAD AND MOM

CONTENTS

PRELUDE

Dear friend,

   The author David James Duncan described the plastic shepherds from those Christmas dioramas of his youth as having "slack-jawed expressions of wonder." There was a time in my life when the stories surrounding the birth of Jesus left me in the same state. However, for some reason or reasons, I lost the eyes to see or the ears to hear, or maybe the heart to wonder. I set out this year (2007) to read them in Eugene Peterson's The Message *in hopes of recapturing a slacked jaw.*

As I read, I was struck by how earthy the stories are; in other words, how utterly human. Even in this day and age of "real" and "authentic," I fear we keep these stories in the realm of card stock and porcelain figurines. If these stories did not happen to flesh and blood and bone and sinew, then we of all people are to be most pitied.

Each entry begins with the passage from The Message, *and I hope you'll take the time to read it. Peterson's renderings of these verses would bleed if you cut them. After each reading, I've written down my reflections: the thoughts, feelings, hopes, and dreams that surfaced as I spent time with the text. I encourage you to approach them not so much to find an answer or respond, but to ponder them in your heart, Mary-like.*

Each reflection is followed by a short prayer. The heart of each prayer is personal, but I've found that what is most personal is most general.

In no way am I indicating that my words are on the level of God's. The readings are divine, my words are earthly. However, I do believe that every once in a while, there is an intersection of the divine with the human, and in those moments something akin to the word incarnation *happens. Incarnation—"God with meat."*

The achingly beautiful sketches are from the hand of the artist Amanda Jolman.

This Advent season I found again a wonder in my jaws. I pray the same for you.

Grace, always grace,
John
December 2007

RECOGNITION

Who on earth saw him first, knowing
truly who he was? Belly to belly, when
John, prophet in utero, distinguished
in the natal soup the fetal bones, the body
curled like a comma, eyes tight, skull
packed with universal wisdom,
this unborn cousin began to dance.

And when she, birth-giver—
her ordinary vision arrowed down between
her legs, through pain and straw, to her son's dark,
slime-streaked hair, to his very skin, red with
the struggle of being born—she lifted him
to her breast, kissed the face of God,
and felt her own heart leap.

—Luci Shaw
Used with permission of the author

One

Speechless

Luke 1.1–22

So many others have tried their hand at putting together a story of the wonderful harvest of Scripture and history that took place among us, using reports handed down by the original eyewitnesses who served this Word with their very lives. Since I have investigated all the reports in close detail, starting from the story's beginning, I decided to write it all out for you, most honorable Theophilus, so you can know beyond the shadow of a doubt the reliability of what you were taught.

During the rule of Herod, King of Judea, there was a priest assigned service in the regiment of Abijah. His name was Zachariah. His wife was descended from the daughters of Aaron. Her name was Elizabeth. Together they lived honorably before God, careful in keeping to the ways of the commandments and enjoying a clear conscience before God. But they were childless because Elizabeth could never conceive, and now they were quite old.

It so happened that as Zachariah was carrying out his priestly duties before God, working the shift assigned to his regiment, it came his one turn in life to enter the sanctuary of God and burn incense. The congregation was gathered and praying outside the Temple at the hour of the incense offering. Unannounced, an angel of God appeared just to the right of the altar of incense. Zachariah was paralyzed in fear.

But the angel reassured him, "Don't fear, Zachariah. Your prayer has been heard. Elizabeth, your wife, will bear a son by you. You are to name him John. You're going to leap like a gazelle for joy, and not only you— many will delight in his birth. He'll achieve great stature with God.

"He'll drink neither wine nor beer. He'll be filled with the Holy Spirit from the moment he leaves his mother's womb. He will turn many sons and daughters of Israel back to their God. He will herald God's arrival in the style and strength of Elijah, soften the hearts of parents to children, *and kindle devout understanding among hardened skeptics—he'll get the people ready for God."*

Zachariah said to the angel, "Do you expect me to believe this? I'm an old man and my wife is an old woman."

But the angel said, "I am Gabriel, the sentinel of God, sent especially to bring you this glad news. But because you won't believe me, you'll be unable to say a word until the day of your son's birth. Every word I've spoken to you will come true on time—God's time."

Meanwhile, the congregation waiting for Zachariah was getting restless, wondering what was keeping him so long in the sanctuary. When he came out and couldn't speak, they knew he had seen a vision. He continued speechless and had to use sign language with the people.

ZACHARIAH

There were a few enjoying this. Earthy old friends.

"At your age you'll need more than an angel's help."

He laughed silently as his head bobbed up and down. True. He had long ago put the dream of children to rest. Now he was being asked to rouse hope.

His hands rose to say, "Enough, my good friends. I'm going home." He rubbed his throat, a gesture that was becoming a habit.

They all stood and walked the aged priest to the door amidst backslaps and more laughter. As he stepped across the doorway, he turned back to wave. A single tear crawled down his cheek. What was this? The corners of his eyes had been silent for years. He thumbed the tear and turned to go.

His skeptic's walk was quick and nervous. He had known her almost all his life, and she him. "Elizabeth of the daughters of Aaron," he used to call her. She would always smile a girl's smile at that address. But that was when they dreamt together. He realized that one day he must have stopped hoping, the day she became just "Elizabeth." Another tear. He rubbed his throat.

His pace slowed as a grin lined his face. "Elizabeth, your wife, will bear a son by you. You are to name him John ... many will delight in his birth." He stopped in the middle of the path and looked heavenward. He mouthed words only the Mighty One could hear: "Who am I that you are mindful of me? Why should you touch her womb in these old days with new life? What kind of man-child is this to be born of her, this one named 'John'?"

He rubbed his whiskered throat, then placed both hands on his broad hips and began to laugh. The boys playing in the street heard nothing. Senile old man. Zachariah's thoughts returned to earth as he eyed the boys. "My son will soften your parents' hearts to you. My son. He will be great. My son. John." Another tear. "The angel told me so."

He resumed his walk, quickly, hopefully. He had to get home. He had signed, "I'll only be gone a little while." She'd worry if he was gone too long. He knew this, for he knew her, and she him. When evening came, he would lie with her. She would welcome an old priest's advances because she was ever hopeful. He knew this. She was "Elizabeth of the daughters of Aaron," and she would bear his son.

He saw her in the distance, sweeping. She saw him
and waved. A girl's smile was on her face. Another tear
on his.

Do You expect me to believe this?

Mighty One, please forgive my doubts.
I realize it should be different, but
there are days when "I told you so"
is simply not enough. Hope has
been deferred so many times.

I know it's an evil generation that
seeks for a sign, but I'm not a
generation, Lord. I am just one
and my heart has grown cold. Melt
me so that a tear might fall - not
a number of them, but just one.

Sincerely,

John

Two

Carrying John

Luke 1.23–25

When the course of his priestly assignment was completed, he went back home. It wasn't long before his wife, Elizabeth, conceived. She went off by herself for five months, relishing her pregnancy. "So, this is how God acts to remedy my unfortunate condition!" she said.

ELIZABETH

People had known her as a woman who lived honorably before God, careful in her keeping of the commandments. She had known herself as a woman of sorrows, barren. The only thing she would ever nurse was the grief that she could not bear Zachariah a son. It was her "unfortunate condition."

She had accepted the will of the Mighty One long ago. "Let it be to me," she had prayed when her body no longer bled the blood of life. Those were words familiar to her family. The descendants of Aaron knew God's ways are not our own.

Just the sight of a nursing mother would pick the old wound. A baby's faint cry could cause her to jumble words, forget what she had intended to say. "Please, let it be to me" was the prayer behind the prayer that would not die.

But that was then. Almost five months ago.

Now it was as if she were living in a dream. She had sensed the truth that first morning. Beneath the thickened hips, the coarse hair on her head, and the cracks in her fingernails, life stirred. There had been no immediate proof for the skeptic's mind, only the knowing of a woman that something had changed, something was different. After that the physical evidence came each morning as she dressed. Her belly slowly swelled and her breasts plumped. Her skin remembered a young girl's glow. "So, this is how God acts to remedy my unfortunate condition!" she said.

And he had known that morning as well. He had just come in from relieving himself. Again. For some reason he had not seen her standing there. He went to his chair and sat down and started to rub his throat. Then he saw her. His fingers started to follow their habit, but stopped. He stared at her. And he knew.

She said nothing. He made no gesture. He stood and walked the few steps across the room to her. She noticed the tear that spilled from the old man's eye. He took her hands in his and held them tightly. A familiar gesture: "We can do this." She leaned in to kiss his weathered cheek, and he surprised her by turning his face so their lips met. It was something he used to do when they were young. Surprise. Spring had returned to the winter of their days.

She missed him. But she knew this time away had been necessary. Zachariah had signed, "We can do this," but she knew that some things only a woman can do.

There would be plenty for him to do after the child was born. She needed these days to relish her pregnancy before the Mighty One and to pray for the son of her womb. And Elizabeth of the daughters of Aaron also prayed for her people, for she knew with the knowing of a woman that her son would be indifferent to their tastes. Zachariah's son would speak with a voice her husband knew nothing of. She was carrying "John"—the beloved of God. "Let it be."

So, this is how God acts...

Mighty One, I thought I had become content in all circumstances, but You knew better. Contentment that cancels out hope is merely a mask for resignation.

But it's so late, so much time has passed. I don't know if I can do this. I've lived in winter so long, I'm not sure I know how to act in spring. Give me courage to sleep outside.

Sincerely,

John

THREE

Angelic Visitor

Luke 1.26–38

In the sixth month of Elizabeth's pregnancy, God sent the angel Gabriel to the Galilean village of Nazareth to a virgin engaged to be married to a man descended from David. His name was Joseph, and the virgin's name, Mary. Upon entering, Gabriel greeted her:

> *Good morning!*
> *You're beautiful with God's beauty,*
> *Beautiful inside and out!*
> *God be with you.*

She was thoroughly shaken, wondering what was behind a greeting like
that. But the angel assured her, "Mary, you have nothing to fear. God has
a surprise for you: You will become pregnant and give birth to a son and
call his name Jesus.

> He will be great,
>> be called 'Son of the Highest.'
> The Lord God will give him
>> the throne of his father David;
> He will rule Jacob's house forever—
>> no end, ever, to his kingdom."

Mary said to the angel, "But how? I've never slept with a man."

The angel answered,

> The Holy Spirit will come upon you,
>> the power of the Highest hover over you;
> Therefore, the child you bring to birth
>> will be called Holy, Son of God.

"And did you know that your cousin Elizabeth conceived a son, old as she is? Everyone called her barren, and here she is six months pregnant! Nothing, you see, is impossible with God."

And Mary said,

> Yes, I see it all now:
>> I'm the Lord's maid, ready to serve.
> Let it be with me
>> just as you say.

Then the angel left her.

GABRIEL

The theologians have rendered us mindless God-slaves, wisps of cloudy wings, doing nothing but the bidding of the Mighty One. Theologians. There is so much they do not know.

I found her just as He said she would be found: sitting on her bedding, barefooted, knees pulled up to her chest, arms wrapped tightly around them, chin resting on her knee-tops. I saw why she had gained the favor of the Mighty One. I liked this daughter-of-Eve-to-be-the-mother-of-God.

"But how? I've never slept with a man."

I expected this. But unlike that old priest's, hers was not the doubting of a skeptic but rather the wondering of a child.

"But how? I can't see it."

"The Holy Spirit will come upon you, the power of the Highest hover over you. Mary, you have nothing to fear." The Mighty One had expressly said, "Herald the news, Gabriel. Don't report it." I would have liked to elaborate further, but Mary would have to live out the details of my news in days to come. Truths unlived are not truths.

Then she paused and looked away. I have spoken to many of God's children, and their eyes are always transfixed on me. They should be. I am Gabriel, the sentinel of God. But Mary's gaze wandered for a moment. But what I initially took for a distracted mind was rather a devoted heart.

Her eyes returned to me. "Let it be with me." Ah, the Mighty One had chosen well. Her words were not resigned, but faith-full. The faith of a child. Of such is the Mighty One's kingdom.

"Cousin Elizabeth? Really? *Old* Elizabeth? But how?"

I laughed.

"Nothing, you see, is impossible with God. Mary, you have nothing to fear. I have told you all you need to know for now. You are more ready than you realize, stronger than you know. God is with you. Now I must go."

But I did not want to go. Faith is rare, at least true faith. Yes, the word is often used, but the reality is hard to find. Yet here I found it, in an earthen vessel surrounded by an earthen room. I liked Mary.

I left her just as He said I would: barefooted, sitting on her bedding, knees pulled up to her chest, arms wrapped tightly around them, chin resting on her knee-tops. She looked older now. Human eyes would not recognize this, but mine have seen much.

The Mighty One had revealed glimpses to me, what days ahead would hold for this glorious girl. Her cousin's leaping womb. Joseph's broad shoulders. The back of a borrowed burro. Herod's jealous-red face. The cries of the innocent. The breath of stable animals. The agony of pushing the Mighty One out into this world.

I found myself praying for the favored one. Mary had so much to carry.

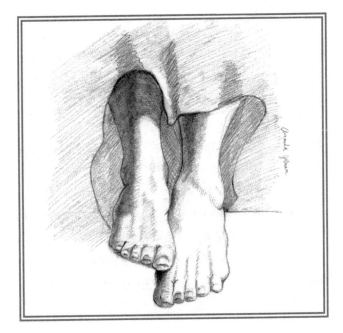

Truths unlived are not truths.

Mighty One, I believe those words, but there are days, many days, when I wish it were not so. The living out of Your truths often involves pain and weariness and wrestling. I fear I've misplaced my childlike faith.

Must it be this way? Yes, I know. During the pain of carrying what You've chosen me to bear, let it be to me. Through the weariness of becoming who You've chosen me to be, let it be to me. In the wrestling of Your must-be-lived truths, let it be to me.

Sincerely,
John

Four

Mothers and Sons

Luke 1.39–56

Mary didn't waste a minute. She got up and traveled to a town in Judah in the hill country, straight to Zachariah's house, and greeted Elizabeth. When Elizabeth heard Mary's greeting, the baby in her womb leaped. She was filled with the Holy Spirit, and sang out exuberantly,

> You're so blessed among women,
>   and the babe in your womb, also blessed!
> And why am I so blessed that
>   the mother of my Lord visits me?

The moment the sound of your
　　greeting entered my ears,
The babe in my womb
　　skipped like a lamb for sheer joy.
Blessed woman, who believed what God said,
　　believed every word would come true!

And Mary said,

I'm bursting with God-news;
I'm dancing the song of my Savior God.
God took one good look at me, and look what happened—
　　I'm the most fortunate woman on earth!
What God has done for me will never be forgotten,
　　the God whose very name is holy, set apart from all others.
His mercy flows in wave after wave
　　on those who are in awe before him.
He bared his arm and showed his strength,
　　scattered the bluffing braggarts.
He knocked tyrants off their high horses,
　　pulled victims out of the mud.

The starving poor sat down to a banquet;
> *the callous rich were left out in the cold.*
He embraced his chosen child, Israel;
> *he remembered and piled on the mercies, piled them*
> *high.*
It's exactly what he promised,
> *beginning with Abraham and right up to now.*

Mary stayed with Elizabeth for three months and then went back to her own home.

ELIZABETH

We were standing in the approach of dusk. I had only just returned to Zachariah's house after my time away. He bent to one knee to rub the good earth.

It's unusual to see someone running in the hill country, especially at this time of day. My first thought was shock. Has something happened? An accident of some kind? Is that a *girl*? What is she saying?

"Zachariah! Zachariah, get up! Someone is coming!"

His voice was silent, but his eyesight was still that of a younger man. He paused and then smiled. His eloquent hands waved my anxiety away. I waited just a moment more. "Mary? Little Mary? Child, what in heaven's name?"

She ran holding her belly, as if carrying something fragile but vital. As she reached me, I took her shoulders: "Child, slow down. What is it?"

She spoke directly to me, but her gaze passed through me. At her first word my son moved violently within me. He has been moving since the beginning; I know he will be born a man of contention. But this was different. It was as if Mary's glad news was a costly pearl a field owner had suddenly come upon, or a poor woman's lost coin that had finally been discovered. It was as if her tidings were confirming the purpose of his life, our lives.

"Here, child. Feel his joy. This one will come first."

The Spirit of the Mighty One warmed me. I took my cousin's face in my calloused hands. I could do nothing but sing:

"Beautiful," the Mighty One says,
"you and the child that you carry."
Yet who am I to sing to you?
Your words roused the wildness
    within,
my son to be born raged with joy.
Faithful Mary. It is very good!

Then Mary spoke:

My heart's cry has been, "Look at me.
    See me. Watch me."
The Mighty One has granted my wish
    and look at me now!
They will talk of what He has done for
    me for generations to come.
Heaven's mercy bathes those who hear
    and obey.
His strength brings the proud to their
    knees.
His compassion raises the poor from
    their knees,

> He sets a table before them in the
>   presence of their enemies.
> No, the Mighty One has not forgotten
>   His Israel.
> His mercies endure forever.
> It is as He has promised from the
>   beginning.
> He is coming!

We suddenly realized our audience: Zachariah. He was standing there watching, listening, silent. My old priest would later tell me that a riderless horse paused in the distance as we sang and spoke that day. The meaning of this he could not say. Nor can I.

"Come, child. You must stay with me. We've much to talk of. Zachariah will inform your mother. All will be well." And so she did, for three months.

His mercies endure forever.

Mighty One, I am not the only one who carries Your promise within. Give me eyes and ears to confirm, and voice to sing. I want to be one of the great witnesses on this earth.

Let my life ring out: THE MIGHTY ONE HAS NOT FORGOTTEN. HIS MERCIES ENDURE FOREVER.

Sincerely,

John

FIVE

The Wild One

Luke 1.57–66

When Elizabeth was full-term in her pregnancy, she bore a son. Her neighbors and relatives, seeing that God had overwhelmed her with mercy, celebrated with her.

On the eighth day, they came to circumcise the child and were calling him Zachariah after his father. But his mother intervened: "No. He is to be called John."

"But," they said, "no one in your family is named that." They used sign language to ask Zachariah what he wanted him named.

Asking for a tablet, Zachariah wrote, "His name is to be John." That took
everyone by surprise. Surprise followed surprise—Zachariah's mouth
was now open, his tongue loose, and he was talking, praising God!

A deep, reverential fear settled over the neighborhood, and in all that
Judean hill country people talked about nothing else. Everyone who heard
about it took it to heart, wondering, "What will become of this child?
Clearly, God has his hand in this."

ZACHARIAH

Even after nine months I was still amazed each time
I saw her. Elizabeth, my wife of many years, pregnant.
How could this be? The angel was right to bind my
tongue. I had lived the psalmist's words: Be quiet and
know that I am God.

The women gathered to help her. Much of this
Elizabeth would do herself; their presence was mainly
ministry. I walked some distance behind the house, but
not so far that I couldn't return in a moment's notice.

Creation seemed quiet, waiting. My wife, however, was not quiet. Her cries and groans filled the stilled air.

"Mighty One, she is my life's love. Give her strength for this moment."

And then the cry of my Elizabeth was replaced by another's. I girded myself and ran. Creation held her tongue no longer. The rocks themselves were singing.

Had I been a younger man, I would have allowed the older women to stop me at the door. But I was not a young man. I had learned they were nine-tenths bluff.

It was as if I stepped into mercy itself. Our eyes met, and my Elizabeth's tongue was also stilled. She spoke with the nod of her head: "He is here." Her tired arms invited me to come and see. And I saw.

※

"No! He is to be called John!" My wife's tone was adamant. It shushed the old women.

The oldest dared to question. "What? There is no 'John' in your family."

Had I been a younger man, I might have tried to soften the moment. But I was not a young man. I motioned for my tablet. My words were pointed: "His name is to be John." As I wrote, I remembered the moment the angel grasped my throat. And suddenly he let go. "His name is to be John," I said. "His name is to be John," I said. "His name is—" I stopped mid-sentence.

Silence.

The air was cut by the laughter of my old hope-filled wife. And suddenly everyone was laughing and praising God. Most of all, me. I rubbed my throat, as I had for months. And then I wiped my eyes.

The days and weeks that followed were mixed with fear and wonder. Although joy resounded through this hill country, there was also something else in the air—a question, one asked by everyone, including me: "What will become of this child?"

What will become of this child?

Mighty One, for me, for all of us,
give strength for this moment.
Something is struggling to be born in
us today. But as with any birth,
we are filled with fear and wonder.

Some births bring peace. Some bring
a sword. We never know what will
become of Your dreams.

Sincerely,

John

Six

Prophet

Luke 1.67–80

Then Zachariah was filled with the Holy Spirit and prophesied,

> *Blessed be the Lord, the God of Israel;*
> > *he came and set his people free.*
> *He set the power of salvation in the center of our lives,*
> > *and in the very house of David his servant,*
> *Just as he promised long ago*
> > *through the preaching of his holy prophets:*
> *Deliverance from our enemies*
> > *and every hateful hand;*

Mercy to our fathers,
  as he remembers to do what he said he'd do,
What he swore to our father Abraham—
  a clean rescue from the enemy camp,
So we can worship him without a care in the world,
  made holy before him as long as we live.

And you, my child, "Prophet of the Highest,"
  will go ahead of the Master to prepare his ways,
Present the offer of salvation to his people,
  the forgiveness of their sins.
Through the heartfelt mercies of our God,
  God's Sunrise will break in upon us,
Shining on those in the darkness,
  those sitting in the shadow of death,
Then showing us the way, one foot at a time,
  down the path of peace.

The child grew up, healthy and spirited. He lived out in the desert until the day he made his prophetic debut in Israel.

ZACHARIAH

Elizabeth gave birth. Now it was my turn. It was as if nine months of stored-up speech were coming out all at once; I could not stop. The Mighty One was pulling the words from my lips. I lifted my arms in the priestly manner:

> Blessings to Israel's God;
> He came, He saw, He delivered.
> We've had salvation dropped in our
>   laps,
> right here, in David's house.
> His weeping, preaching wild men
> promised this long ago:
> A table in the presence of our
>   enemies.
> Have mercy on us, Mighty One,
> as you are mindful of your promises.
> It all started with Abraham,
> and the great rescue.

> We worship you now in spirit and in
>   truth;
> nothing can separate us from your
>   love.

Then I took my son from Elizabeth. Had I been a younger man, I would have let his mother continue to nuzzle him. But I was not a younger man. I remembered the angel's words: "He'll achieve great stature with God. But do not neglect the fathering simply because you are old. He must be fathered." I raised my son as a priest raises an offering. Everyone in the room was expectant. My words were loud and strong:

> John, my son, Elijah reborn,
> you must go first, scout the way.
> You will cry out, "forgiveness,"
> but you cannot make them take it.
> The Mighty One is merciful,
> the clouds will break, the dawn is
>   coming.

The Life-Light will blaze in the
    darkness,
no more night.
Peace on earth. Peace for us all.

The room was deathly still, no one moved. My son began to wrestle against his blanket. I pulled him close and prophesied directly into his eyes. Perhaps the others in the room thought the angel had once again bound my tongue, for my lips were moving, but no sound was heard. But the last nine months had taught me much of the prayer of the heart. I knew what I was doing. Besides, these words were not for them; they were for John:

I have dreamed of you, my beloved.
    You will be so much more than me.

Elizabeth broke the silence by reaching for our son. I returned him to her embrace. She would later tell me of a wildness she saw in my eyes that day. It scared her.

John grew strong, always running. "Exuberant!" a neighbor declared. He seemed to live in the margins, somewhere between this world and the next.

I was not there the day he ran toward his destiny. I had passed years earlier. But I watched and voiced a prayer:

"Ready yourselves, Israel. My son, John, is coming."

Ready your selves...

Mighty One, help me to remember that
I am only to share what I've seen and
heard; convincing and persuading is
up to You. You are the One who draws
the hearts of men. I can offer, but
I cannot make anyone take.

You are the Mighty One, not me.

Sincerely,

John

Interlude

We who have known the touch of
flesh and the shape of bones ...

—Madeleine L'Engle, "To a Long-Loved Love"

She tries to keep a faithful posture, but the late-term heaviness of her breasts is too much for a girl's musculature. Bowing over her taut belly, she appears turned in on herself. She squeezes her eyes tight, trying desperately to remember the angel's visit and the song it birthed: *"My soul glorifies the Lord ..."*

"Did that really happen?" she wonders. "Was I only dreaming?"

A contraction seizes the slight frame, and her questions are physically answered. The Mighty One has not chosen to part the waters or stop the sun. No, He has chosen to overshadow her, bodily. At this moment she would prefer a floating axe-head or a ram in the thicket, anything but the deep place within. But the angel said time was now full and God desired to be born in us.

"Let it be, then."

Each tightening atop the burro causes her to lose balance. She reaches out to stabilize herself and finds the shoulder of her Joseph. He has steadied her all along the way. Joseph. God's midwife. Their eyes meet and she wishes for the strength of his words: "Just a little farther, my love." But her wish remains a wish.

He has been quiet most of the day. Her growing has been evident to the eyes of more than she cared for. His gestation has been inward. The Mighty One desires to be born in his words, redeeming the silence of Adam. He shakes the memory of the garden from his con-sciousness. "I'm sorry, my Mary. Just a little farther."

She places a hand on the side of her belly. An unborn heel is making it hard for her to breathe. She, too, thinks of the garden and the promise of a heel bruised. She leans back, inhaling, and rubs the rise beneath her skin. "A little farther, baby."

She remembers another day of difficult breathing. As her Joseph led her from the house, her first love cried the tears of a boy. Her father's tears mingled with her own so that she thought she'd drown. Leaving the earthly for the divine is never easy.

"Oh, Abba."

Another contraction dissolves the farewell memory. The burro's ears frame their destination: Bethlehem, the House of Bread. They pass an old crone hobbling on tired legs. Her soul is bent from weeping for her children. Rachel lifts her gaze to the mother of God. As their eyes meet, Mary hears the unspoken grace: "You can do this, favored one. A little farther. Just a little farther."

Seven

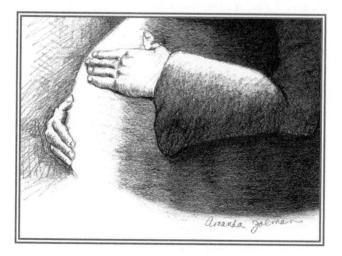

The Father

Psalm 29.3–10

GOD *thunders across the waters,*
Brilliant, his voice and his face, streaming brightness—
GOD, *across the flood waters.*

GOD's *thunder tympanic,*
GOD's *thunder symphonic.*

GOD's *thunder smashes cedars,*
GOD *topples the northern cedars.*

The mountain ranges skip like spring colts,
The high ridges jump like wild kid goats.

GOD's *thunder spits fire.*
GOD *thunders, the wilderness quakes;*
He makes the desert of Kadesh shake.

GOD's *thunder sets the oak trees dancing*
A wild dance, whirling; the pelting rain strips their branches.
We fall to our knees—we call out, "Glory!"

Above the floodwaters is GOD's *throne*
from which his power flows,
from which he rules the world.

I AM. I am the Mighty One. Even though I AM beyond time, I have been and will be in all times: tomorrow, the now, even long ago.

Humans have been shouting their question for millennia: *Why in God's name won't you show up?* They say it when the moment seems to demand a force to do good:

If you are God, then do something. But to *show up* in those moments would be to come in your name, not Mine. My ways are not your ways.

It was no different on the night in question. The weary world pleaded for power. I chose weakness.

I had shaped Mary in her mother's womb, fashioned her from nothing into something. I had crafted her frame so as to support the weight of her life. Her days had been prepared before she lived even one. I had gone before her, been behind, and on all sides. I am the Mighty One. And I was with her then as she writhed Love to life.

She was brave. Only Joseph by her side, a cramped place to give birth, noise everywhere. And more. As she screamed out in pain, the Deceiver stood ready to devour My Son. The heavens shook with war. Michael and his angels reeled. *Mighty One, do something!*

I AM.

I had given My word: *You'll give birth to your babies in pain.* Mary held fast to hers: *Let it be to me.* And so it was.

Joseph thought Mary pushed. The truth is, she shook and rocked on exhausted knees as I held her by My strong right arm and the brightness grew until she could bear no more. Time pulled eternity from the womb of a girl, and bloodstained Love spilled on the hay.

Bravely done, My child. It is only just beginning.

Always...

Mighty One, I know of my own
pleadings for You to do something!
My life's story tells me that You
have, are, and will. But it's always
in Your name. I do want it that
way, even when I scream to the
contrary.

Sincerely,

John

EIGHT

The Son

John 17.1–5

Jesus said these things. Then, raising his eyes in prayer, he said:

> *Father, it's time.*
> *Display the bright splendor of your Son*
> *So the Son in turn may show your bright splendor.*
> *You put him in charge of everything human*
> *So he might give real and eternal life to all in his charge.*
> *And this is the real and eternal life:*
> *That they know you,*
> *The one and only true God,*

And Jesus Christ, whom you sent.
I glorified you on earth
By completing down to the last detail
What you assigned me to do.
And now, Father, glorify me with your very own splendor,
The very splendor I had in your presence
Before there was a world.

My Father said: *My Son, it's time. Time for My love for You to be among them. Time for My splendor to be heard with their ears, seen with their eyes, felt with their hands. For You, it will be a difficult splendor.*

I said: *Not My will, but Yours. Let it be to Me.*

The only way was to trust My Father. As angels stood aghast, I let go the privileges of deity and was swept into the desire of the Mighty One. The glory overshadowed a young girl, and I emptied Myself. I heard Him say, *I will never leave you, My Son. Never.*

And then the darkness.

As I floated in her water, Mary brooded over Me with songs. It was comforting. But then her voice stilled,

her heart raced, her breathing came labored. The darkness thinned, the light grew; something was about to
change. Behind it all, a voice faint but unmistakable,
like whispered joy: *My Son, it's time.*

Never...

Mighty One, I need to hear these words today: I WILL NEVER LEAVE YOU. I don't care how they come, just please send them, speak them. I feel alone and cold, overshadowed. Please remind me that You are here.

Sincerely,

John

NINE

Birth

Luke 2.1–7

About that time Caesar Augustus ordered a census to be taken throughout the Empire. This was the first census when Quirinius was governor of Syria. Everyone had to travel to his own ancestral hometown to be accounted for. So Joseph went from the Galilean town of Nazareth up to Bethlehem in Judah, David's town, for the census. As a descendant of David, he had to go there. He went with Mary, his fiancée, who was pregnant.

While they were there, the time came for her to give birth. She gave birth to a son, her firstborn. She wrapped him in a blanket and laid him in a manger, because there was no room in the hostel.

JOSEPH

Do you know who most reminds me of me these days? Old Job, the faithful. Old Job, the sufferer. He had lived according to the will of the Mighty One, yet all was taken away. I, too, had lived by the commandments. No one had forced me; it was my decision. Yet all seemed taken away.

Before *that* dream I'd had other dreams. Dreams without angels in them. Visions of Mary and children. The children would grow strong and devout, and Mary and I would ease into a cranky elegance. We would live a well-ordered life. Then all those dreams were snatched away.

In the days just after Mary confirmed what I'd been told, I thought of the lines from Job's drama: "Curse God and die." If you do not believe there were moments when that invitation was tempting, then you make me out to be something I am not. I am not an angel or one of the lesser gods. I am a man. This was not the life I planned.

But curse the Mighty One? I could not. My ordered life? A memory. The control I'd long worked to establish?

Gone. In truth it may never have been there, but I thought it was, lived like it was. My reputation among family and friends? Stained. What kind of story was this I had fallen into?

But curse the Mighty One? I would not, for I'd had *that* dream. A carpenter works with what he can see and feel; a corner angle and the heft of wood. But here I was chasing a dream. The afternoon of my life looked nothing like the morning.

So on to Bethlehem it was. We had known the census was coming, but the timing was horrible. While we were there, Mary went into labor. It was time. In that moment my dreams of always being able to provide for my wife were snatched as well. I could not even find a decent place for her to deliver the child. Voices of shame raged against me almost daily: "You are *just* a carpenter, Joseph. Who are you to accompany the only begotten of God? He is not even your son. Why are you walking away from all you've built *just* because of a dream?"

You must know I tried. But there were things I could not make happen. I can make about anything. But wood is not the medium of the Mighty One.

"No room."

"We have no room."

"What, are you blind? Do you not see all the people?"

"Look, son. I see your need. There is room in my stable. It's all I can offer you. Take it. You should have made better plans."

I am dismayed by the way that night is remembered. There are those who tell the story as if it were a production, a staged affair. That is blasphemous. It was no production. It was a birth. I was scared. She was scared. He was Mary's first. I had witnessed cattle being born, but never a child. There were no bright lights. The animals did not move on cue. No one sang.

He came as all men come, bathed in the lifeblood of His mother. His conception was divine. His birth was of the earth.

It was my responsibility, one of the few things I could do. I raised the knife and freed Him from her. I, Joseph the carpenter, released the Son of the Mighty One into this world. My knife was dull; it took two tries. The blood from the cord wet my forearms. So much blood. So much blood.

Mary wrapped Him as if she'd wrapped newborns before. But she was exhausted.

"Joseph, I must rest. Here, take Him."

The Scriptures say that God blessed Job's later life more than his earlier life. He ended up with sheep, camels, oxen, donkeys, sons and daughters, and grandchildren.

I could only hope my story would conclude like that of the old sufferer. The dream I chased had my back against a stable wall, my fiancée asleep in blood-red hay, skittish sheep and oxen as onlookers, and my hands filled with a Son not my own.

"What do I do now? I am just a carpenter."

MARY

The time was coming for me to give birth.

Joseph pleaded, "Mary, stay and rest. I'll just be a moment."

But I would not. I was afraid. God's sentinel had told me that I would be the mother of the hoped-for

One. Courage arose in me that I knew not, and I said,
"Let it be to me."

But that was nine months past. A glorious beginning had leveled off to an ordinary middle. There were
no more angels or prophecies or leaping wombs. There
were only crowds and noise. And fear.

"Joseph, I will be fine. I want to walk a little. Maybe
it will hasten the time. Just let it be."

Tenderness. The ability to be still, to pause, to make
space for the Mighty One's hand. It is a trait not always
seen in the sons of Adam. But it accurately describes the
life of Joseph. It was Joseph's gift to me in that town of
no room.

We walked only steps from the stable. He had to do
one last thing concerning the registration in his ancestral
hometown. But we never made it to the official's desk.

We were standing in a line of six or seven people.
Joseph was in front of me, and I stood behind with my
forehead pressed between his shoulder blades. I had not
been able to see my feet in months, but suddenly I felt
them. Wet and warm. A dog sitting nearby came and
licked the sand.

Joseph must have sensed the dog and turned to shoo him away, but he stayed his hand when he saw the ground beneath my feet.

Tenderness knew that Quirinius did not govern moments such as these. Joseph's ropy arms encircled me and led my shuffling, wet feet from our place in line. We took a journey back to the stable that made the trip to Bethlehem pale.

After two steps a tightening bent me double. This was not like the earlier stirrings in my belly. When I was able to resume walking, the stillness caught us unawares. All the activity around us had ceased: the exchange of census information, the men talking, the dog licking the watered sand. Everyone and everything stared at us— tenderly, I thought. I believe both man and beast knew, if only for a moment, that the time was coming.

Joseph picked me up. With one arm around my waist, he bent and cradled my knees with the other. He rose and began to carry me. I do not know how this man did many of the things he did, things unrecorded for history. I am only thankful he did them.

Gabriel had said, "Mary, you have nothing to fear."

As I lay on my back, I searched the openings of light in the roof for an angelic return. I needed to hear those words again. But I could not. My hearing was dulled, but I smelled everything. Wet hay. Joseph's sweat. The dung of oxen and sheep. Someone frying bread nearby. And I smelled my own fear.

I felt everything as well. The hay pricking my calves. Joseph's hand in the small of my back, steadying me. The body heat of animals nearby. The brooding between my legs. And the fear.

"Joseph, help me to my knees. Just do it."

When you are afraid, you reach out for the familiar. In that moment I wanted to feel my knees. When Gabriel first stood before me, I was holding my knees. Now that the time was coming, I wanted to feel them once more, get my bearings. If this Son would truly hold throne of David, then I would birth Him on bended knee.

A part of me had expected divine intervention, a lightening of the burden of birth. But it never came. For the Son of the Highest to also be the Son of Man, He had to be tested in all ways as we are. Including in His birth.

I wished for my mother, for her voice to say "breathe" and "push." Joseph didn't know what women say. I pushed.

"Let ... it ..."

"I'm here, Mary. Just a little more."

"Let ... it ... be ... to ..."

"His head, Mary. I see His head."

"Let ... it ... be ... to ... me."

Then a sound that pierced my heart. His cry.

Still on my knees I reached between my legs and raised my newborn son for those gathered there: "Truly, this is the Son of God."

No room.

Mighty One, this is not the life I planned. I had heard Your ways were not our ways, but I really had no idea. The road I had hoped to be straight has been a crooked little path. The hopes and dreams of my youth have faded.

But, there is something now that remains, something truer about me. And about You. This is not the life I planned. Thank You for my life.

Sincerely,
John

TEN

Angels and Relatives

Luke 2.8–20

There were sheepherders camping in the neighborhood. They had set night watches over their sheep. Suddenly, God's angel stood among them and God's glory blazed around them. They were terrified. The angel said, "Don't be afraid. I'm here to announce a great and joyful event that is meant for everybody, worldwide: A Savior has just been born in David's town, a Savior who is Messiah and Master. This is what you're to look for: a baby wrapped in a blanket and lying in a manger."

At once the angel was joined by a huge angelic choir singing God's praises:

> *Glory to God in the heavenly heights,*
> *Peace to all men and women on earth who please him.*

As the angel choir withdrew into heaven, the sheepherders talked it over. "Let's get over to Bethlehem as fast as we can and see for ourselves what God has revealed to us." They left, running, and found Mary and Joseph, and the baby lying in the manger. Seeing was believing. They told everyone they met what the angels had said about this child. All who heard the sheepherders were impressed.

Mary kept all these things to herself, holding them dear, deep within herself. The sheepherders returned and let loose, glorifying and praising God for everything they had heard and seen. It turned out exactly the way they'd been told!

BENJAMIN THE SHEPHERD

Just a kid. He knew little about sheep and less about life. But my dying brother's request had been, "Make sure my son sees more than me." A year later I was still my brother's son's keeper.

It was the boy's watch. But I would wager he was asleep. Again.

"Benjamin, your nephew's waiting for his lullaby," said one of the men. I was grateful their jesting stayed innocent. He was just a kid.

As I walked through them to rouse him once again, there it was. Not my nephew. Something I'd never seen before. It was as if the sun had suddenly risen in the middle of our fire. As my brother had drawn his last breaths, he had talked of angels. Beautiful. Unsettling. Now I felt as if death had found me as well.

It spoke. We could hardly bear the sound.

"Don't be afraid. It has just happened. A great and joyful moment the world has been waiting for. A newborn Savior cries in Bethlehem, our Messiah and Master. You must search for the baby. Look in the manger."

Then we saw the rest of them. If death had indeed found me, it was a good death. Even brighter and more beautiful. The fear was gone.

They sang, and we could hardly bear their joy. They sang a song of the exiles, now suddenly home.

> Glory to God above.
> Peace to all below.

The night swallowed their joy. Our fire still burned. And then we began to run. It was foolish to leave the sheep and the fire, but everything was different now. Sheep were sheep. This was something else.

How we found them, I do not know. But there was much about that night beyond my knowing. There they were. She was sleeping. He was holding the child. We approached and he rose to greet us.

"Is He the One?"

"Yes. He is called Jesus. The Savior. Let me tell you the story."

She woke and smiled at us. Her hands were folded on her chest, as if in prayer, as if holding something deep within. He called her "Mary."

We returned to find some of the sheep had strayed. It did not matter. My nephew stirred the embers, and our fire blazed once more. We stood in the circle of its warmth and talked the quiet talk of shepherds. My brother's son was rattling on just like a kid. I heard again my best friend's dying wish: "Benjamin, make sure he sees more than me."

He has, brother. He has.

BENJAMIN'S NEPHEW

The fool has said there is no God.

I was a fool. But I did not care. I had prayed to the God of Israel to spare my father's life. His fever came suddenly, in the spring of my eleventh year. Friends and neighbors surrounded him and prayed.

I prayed too. And my father died. And I became a fool.

My uncle vowed to care for me. His vow led me into long days and cold nights tending sheep. In the days when a boy most needs a father, I got an uncle and a group of shepherds. No, there was no God.

Most days I did not tend sheep. I sulked. Occasionally one of the others would ask, "What's wrong with you?" I had no words for it, but I lived with the sense that people or things could be lost at any moment. I was afraid.

It was my watch. I knew my uncle would be coming by soon to check up on me, so I paced to stay awake. And then it was as if the fire that kept the other shepherds warm gave birth to something beyond the world of sheep and stone.

"Don't be afraid. It has just happened ..."

I was twenty paces from the group, yet the words scoured my brain. My father had spoken of angels, at the end. I hadn't believed him.

And then we were standing in front of a man holding a newborn baby and a woman asleep in bloody hay.

The words of young fools are often dismissed. But I do not care. Not to tell of this would be foolish indeed.

As I looked at the child, I felt that something lost had been found. Not my father; I still ache for his face. No, this was something deeper that had been lost, probably before my father's fever. Maybe even before I was born. I'm not sure.

I asked the man if he was the baby's father. The man paused and said, "No. God is His father. But I am keeping watch over Him for now."

As the man told his tale, my uncle pulled me to his chest. I was amazed at the texture of his arm and the smell of his body; I might as well have been standing by my father. Here were gifts I found that had been there all along. Looking at the baby, I found I had eyes to see and ears to hear.

The man looked at Benjamin and asked me, "Is this your father?"

I said, "No. But he is keeping watch."

The man smiled at me.

AN ANGEL

To say that His birth was *opposed* is to touch the limits of mortal language. The Mighty One has been hated since the pride of the bright one led many away. Your word *war* comes close, but even then, believe me, you have no idea.

We sang that night as we had never sung before. Those shepherds believed they were the primary audience. True, they were important—the Mighty One has always favored the lowly. But there was much going on that night. The other reason we sang in the fields was to hallow the ground where Rachel would weep over her sons. There the graves would be dug, the graves for the little boys of Bethlehem.

Herod's rage soon stripped dozens of firstborns from the breasts that nursed them. Those so fresh from God, so quickly silenced. Slaughtered like animals. So much blood.

The town had no room for Mary, as Herod's heart had no room for another king. He would not share his glory. He would destroy this threat if he had to go through all the firstborns in the kingdom.

Although we do not exist in time, there are moments when the affairs of earth are hard to endure. Even angels desire vengeance.

"Vengeance is Mine," declared the Mighty One. "Justice is coming. I need you to sing."

And so we sang:

> Glory to God in the heavenly heights,
> Peace to all men and women on earth
>   who please Him.

And Gabriel said, "Again, louder."

We sang again.

"Again, louder. The Mighty One said, 'Prepare the way!'"

What the shepherds heard as an anthem, the innocents would hear as a lullaby. We sang as we had never sung before. A song to bring Him into the world, a song to guide them safely from it, and a song to help her endure it:

Glory to God in the heavenly heights,
  (Fly, fly to the breast of the Father,
  This wrong will be righted,
  Jesus is here.)

Peace to all men and women on earth
  who please Him.
    (Rest, rest in the arms of the
      Father,
    His fury remembers,
    His love holds you dear.)

Many do not sing of this horror at Christmas. That is understandable; it was an unspeakable deed. But I remind you that His birth was opposed. You have no idea.

Vengeance is Yours.

I think I want justice, so my
thoughts are of vengeance. But I know
it's mercy I want and need. The
world does too.
Grant me the courage to drop my fists
and sing.

Sincerely,

John

ELEVEN

The Dreamer

Luke 2.21–35

When the eighth day arrived, the day of circumcision, the child was named Jesus, the name given by the angel before he was conceived.

Then when the days stipulated by Moses for purification were complete, they took him up to Jerusalem to offer him to God as commanded in God's Law: "Every male who opens the womb shall be a holy offering to God," and also to sacrifice the "pair of doves or two young pigeons" prescribed in God's Law.

In Jerusalem at the time, there was a man, Simeon by name, a good man,
a man who lived in the prayerful expectancy of help for Israel. And the
Holy Spirit was on him. The Holy Spirit had shown him that he would
see the Messiah of God before he died. Led by the Spirit, he entered the
Temple. As the parents of the child Jesus brought him in to carry out the
rituals of the Law, Simeon took him into his arms and blessed God:

> *God, you can now release your servant;*
>> *release me in peace as you promised.*
> *With my own eyes I've seen your salvation;*
>> *it's now out in the open for everyone to see:*
> *A God-revealing light to the non-Jewish nations,*
>> *and of glory for your people Israel.*

Jesus' father and mother were speechless with surprise at these words.
Simeon went on to bless them, and said to Mary his mother,

> *This child marks both the failure and*
>> *the recovery of many in Israel,*
> *A figure misunderstood and contradicted—*
>> *the pain of a sword-thrust through you—*

But the rejection will force honesty,
    as God reveals who they really are.

JOSEPH

"A holy offering to the Mighty One is every son of Adam born. As are you, my son." Father Abraham had spoken those words to Isaac, the son of promise. Jesse had spoken them to David, our greatest king. Amon had spoken them to Josiah, the boy who found the Law. Matthan had spoken them to Jacob, my gentle father. And Jacob had spoken them to me, almost every day.

How I wished my father was there to see all this. He often walked in my dreams, as if waiting for something. Or someone.

The days of purification were complete and the old ways had to be honored.

"Mary, are you ready? Jerusalem waits."

"Yes, let it be. You've taken care of the doves?"

"All will be well, Mary."

When we entered the temple courts, it was as if I were seeing a ghost. This man could be my father's twin. He stared into my eyes. His tired, expectant eyes smiled. And then he gathered his robe and began to run toward us like some heartsick father at the sight of his prodigal.

I reached out to slow her. "Mary, wait."

He ran to us and stopped. Then he looked at the child. He raised his hands, asking to hold Him. His hands were the hands of my father, Jacob. Gentle, but strong. Trustworthy.

I said, "Mary, give Him to me."

Her resistance was a mother's. She searched my eyes for answers.

"All will be well, Mary."

She slowly handed Jesus to me. And I slowly offered Jesus to him. I am a simple man. I know little of that beyond the good earth. But this I believe with all I am: The Mighty One knows our dreams and seeks to redeem them. It was as if I placed the child in my father's hands, as if he were seeing all this.

He raised Jesus and began to speak:

> A holy offering to the Mighty One is
>   every son of Adam born.
> But this one is the begotten of God.
> This one is Israel's salvation.
> This one is the light of the world.
> I am released from my dreams.
> Now I can go in peace.

I could tell that Mary had no idea what was happening before her eyes. Moments such as these would be long pondered in her heart before they were distilled in words. But I knew. Prayerful Simeon had seen the salvation of the Lord. And my father had too.

The one with gentle hands then turned his attention to Mary:

> This one reveals the desolation and
>   the consolation.
> Listen to my words, favored one:
> This child will rend your heart.

He then turned to me, but said nothing. He simply handed Jesus back to me. Our hands brushed in the exchange. We both paused. And then he walked out of our lives.

Mary is and always will be the favored one. But I have known moments of favor as well. I am Joseph, the son of Jacob. My life, like my father's, is a holy offering to the child I now hold.

SIMEON

I am remembered as a good man. *A good man?* Scripture is too kind. Only the Mighty One is good.

He had shown me on more than one occasion that I would see His Messiah. *How* did He show me, you ask? Ah, I learned long ago not to give away all my gold. You'll just have to trust *a good man.*

After seeing His salvation, I would be released in peace. My years of late had not been peaceful. It wasn't so much a lack of peace within myself, but an absence of it in the world. A darkness was descending, something deeper than the usual fallen ways of man. People were quick to anger and slow to forgive, if they forgave at all. Maybe I was just old and it had always been that way. But it seemed exaggerated.

I would arise each morning with a prayerful expectancy; such was my love for Israel. I always thought it akin to what Father Noah must have felt. The waiting. Waiting for the waters to subside. Waiting to feel the promise. The bow in the sky is one thing. The ground beneath your feet is another. I was all too ready to hold the promise.

Then one morning it was as if the dove returned with the sprig in her mouth. I made my way to the temple—asking, seeking, knocking. And I saw him. Not the child, but the man. His face gave him away. It wasn't his hair or cheekbones or beard; no, it was a look, the look of a man released in peace. I wanted his look.

This peaceful man took the bundle from her and handed it to me. I do not have words to describe the anxiety within me at that moment. To see the child would release me. There is safety in years of prayerful expectancy; you can always say, "I'm still waiting." But when the wait is over, everything changes. You are then released into what's next, the unknown.

I unswaddled His face and felt as if I looked into mercy itself. I held the solid ground of the Mighty One's promise in my hands. I raised Him like a bow in the sky:

> A holy offering to the Mighty One is
>   every son of Adam born.
> But this one is the begotten of God ...
> Now I can go in peace.

I could go in peace. But not her. She would have to wait. I did not want to speak these words to her, but I did: "This child will rend your heart." She seemed to know this before I spoke.

I handed Him back to the man. Something beyond the child was exchanged in that moment. Perhaps the child bridged time and healed a hidden wound. I don't know how to say it.

I turned and walked into the crowd.

Time did not cease after Father Noah felt the ground. He continued to live. As did I.

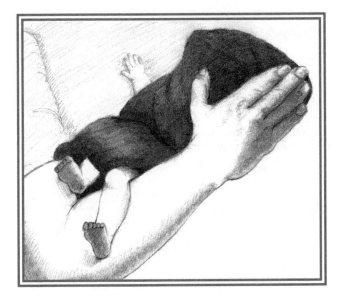

All will be well.

Mighty One, I know those four words from when I was a child, days when dreams first showed themselves, days when I first reached to take Your hand. I believed them.

But now, as a man, I fear I've put away the childlike with the childish. Can dreams really come true? Help my unbelief.

Sincerely,

John

TWELVE

Jerusalem's Freedom

Luke 2.36–40

Anna the prophetess was also there, a daughter of Phanuel from the tribe of Asher. She was by now a very old woman. She had been married seven years and a widow for eighty-four. She never left the Temple area, worshiping night and day with her fastings and prayers. At the very time Simeon was praying, she showed up, broke into an anthem of praise to God, and talked about the child to all who were waiting expectantly for the freeing of Jerusalem.

When they finished everything required by God in the Law, they returned
to Galilee and their own town, Nazareth. There the child grew strong in
body and wise in spirit. And the grace of God was on him.

MARY

I felt aware of everything. Jesus' cheek lay against my
breast. Joseph needed a haircut. Doves were being
bought and sold. Someone coughed or sneezed. It was
too much. I was so young.

We walked into the temple area, and Joseph
stopped me, and this old man came running at us, at
me. Then Joseph asked for Jesus. I placed my life, our
lives, in his hands, and then he handed my son to this ...
this stranger, who then spoke even stranger words that
people pressed in to hear. And Joseph stepped closer to
this man, and suddenly I didn't know what to do with
myself. Until I heard her voice.

She moved through the crowd at a crazed pace, like
someone on fire. Everyone was focused on what this
Simeon was saying, but it was as if she didn't care. The

people seemed to recognize her but not respect her. She appeared to be what is called the starving poor. Her words never ceased: "Jerusalem's freedom has come!"

In all of the activity my senses were absorbing, her words triumphed and stilled me, stabilized me.

"Jerusalem's freedom has come!"

She reached Simeon at the exact moment he lifted Jesus up for all to see. The fire that had been burning in her was suddenly extinguished, and she fell to her knees, not an arm's length from me, and began singing behind Simeon's words. You might think their voices competed, but they did not. It was magnificent. I found myself singing with her, for I'd heard this song before. She was singing *my* song:

> The Mighty One has not forgotten
>   His Israel.
> His mercies endure forever.
> It is as He has promised from the
>   beginning.
> He is here!

The Mighty One's favor comes in unexpected ways. On that day when I felt overwhelmed, felt small in a story so big, He reminded me of my song. My joy. My purpose. My Jesus. I took her hand, and she rose to her tired feet. And we sang. Some looked at us as if we were crazy. When the song ended, she squeezed my hand, and with her other hand she reached and touched the hem of Jesus' blanket. Just the hem.

She leaned in and whispered to me: "Jerusalem's freedom."

I later learned she was a prophetess, the daughter of one Phanuel from the tribe of Asher. She had been a temple fixture for years. Her husband had died years ago, much too soon. Some said she was ruined by grief. Others said she brought all of her sadness to the temple courts and walked it out for over eighty years, pacing and praying and denying herself food and drink and praying and pacing. Most pitied her and called her crazy. Crazy Anna.

But I remember a raging day calmed by a song. Our song. The day when a trembling widow and an anxious girl joined hands and voices. When crazy Anna and crazy Mary sang together in the temple court.

ANNA

The men looked past me. I had found and lost a man, and I had learned to live without them. Women spoke to me with respect but whisper-wondered about unconfessed sins that left me a widow. It was not that my parents or I had sinned, but rather that the Mighty One desired to reveal His glory. But I cared no longer for the eyes of men or the friendships of women.

There was one, though. He was different.

Simeon had seen and spoken to me once: "I am waiting."

That was all. But those words brought comfort to my widow's heart as the hand of a man on his wife's might bring reassurance. To know that there was another who understood me, even in part. That is something many husbands and wives know nothing of.

"I am waiting too."

He smiled. And that was all.

I saw him from time to time in the temple. I was there constantly; he attended as was required. But it was not so much his presence that day that caught my attention, but his pace. Urgent was not a word to describe Simeon. Until that day.

I quickened my pace to get closer to him, and he saw me. And spoke again.

"He is here."

He smiled. And that was all.

Such was my trust in him that I began calling out, "Jerusalem's freedom has come! Jerusalem's freedom!" There are times when you risk all on the words of one who understands. A friend.

As Simeon lifted God's Messiah and spoke, I began to sing. Fasting and praying I had done. Singing I had not. But there are times when you risk all on the hope of One who understands. The Friend.

For two people who had never exchanged more than three little words at a time, you'd have thought we had rehearsed this moment for years. Simeon's speech welled up from deep within. My song came from her, the overshadowed, anxious girl:

> The Mighty One has not forgotten
>   His Israel.
> His mercies endure forever.
> It is as He has promised from the
>   beginning.
> He is here!

I reached in to touch the child and touched wonder itself. The glory of God.

I squeezed the girl's hand and was released in peace.

In unexpected ways....

Mighty One, I often feel small
in a story so big. But I know
the play goes on. And I am asked,
"What will your part be?"

Forgive my diminishment of myself.
And keep me from the belittling of others.
You are Emmanuel — God with us,
God with me.

Sincerely,

John

CODA

Dear friend,

There is a saying that has gained a considerable following: *It's not about you.* The follow-up to this saying goes like this: *It's all about God.* I hope you've felt in these narratives that because of who HE IS, the Mighty One, it can be both—all about Him and all about you. In a way, in the spiritual life, it's always about you.

In that moment when the angel grasped Zachariah's throat, it was all about him. The second when Mary first saw Gabriel in her room, it was all about her. The day Elizabeth groaned John the Baptizer into this world, it was all about her. And in all of those moments and seconds and days, it was also all about Him.

Some would say a perspective like that leads to arrogance. Some say a lot of things. My friend, there is an "arrogance of belonging" that reveals hearts fully attuned to the moment and fully engaged in the story in which they find themselves. It looks like arrogance, I'll give you that. But upon deeper reflection, it shows that in the grand play, each one has been given a part. The question is, "How will you play it?"

These wonder-filled characters played their parts well. I pray you won't diminish the part you've been given. Remember, the Mighty One's favor comes in unexpected ways.

Grace, always grace,

John

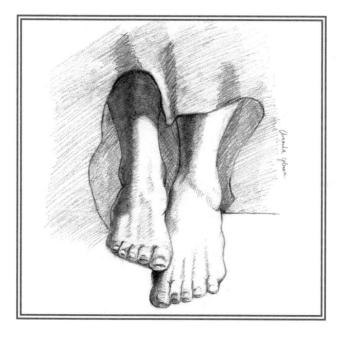

To view additional sketches or inquire about artwork,
visit www.AmandaJolman.com.

WORDS OF GRATITUDE

There are moments you sit up straight in your chair and realize how many people have contributed to the things you sometimes foolishly believe you did on your own. I'm sitting up straight as I type these names:

Kathy Helmers, you first heard these in sermon form and encouraged me to have them published. I'm forever grateful.

Special agent Joel Kneedler. I'm thankful I could become one of your first clients. That way, someday, we can use phrases like "remember when" and chew on toothpicks and stuff.

Don Pape, Terry Behimer, and the rest of my compadres at David C. Cook Publishing. Your willingness to roll the dice on me, not only as an editor, but moreover as an author, continues to amaze me. Y'all are the absolute berries! And Amy, great job on the cover!

Amanda Jolman, artist in classical training, your work has spoken to me since I first saw a sketch in shadowy Shove Chapel. Thanks for being willing to look into these words and give them shape.

Karen Lee-Thorp, you were the editor this project needed. God is good about seeing to details like that. Many, many thanks!

Luci Shaw, thank you for blessing this book with your poem "Recognition" and for your editorial suggestions.

Rich "Bo" Murray, you were there in Santa Fe when the words started falling out of my head on the page. You told me I could write. And I believed you.

Dad and Mom, you always made Christmas special. In fact you still do. Your encouragement in everything I've tried means more than you'll ever know.

Will, Sarah, and Abbey. Only God knows how much I love you.

Meredith, you fell in love with a dreamer. Common sense says avoid such people. Thanks for not paying attention to common sense. I love you back.

And Lord, Your infinitely tender hand continues to leave me a man undone. Simply undone.